CU00704566

First published in Great Britain by
Methanol Press: 2 Tidy Street Brighton East Sussex BN1 4EL

Published to accompany British Speedway

For a complete catalogue of current and forthcoming publications please write to the address above,
or visit our website at www.methanolpress.com or email info@methanolpress.com

ISBN 978-0-9553103-2-4

A catalogue for this book is available from the British Library

Thanks: Michael Payne, Graham Russel, Gerry Kelly, Caroline Tidmarsh, The Reverend Michael
Whawell, Julie Martin, Billy Jenkins, Sheila Le-Sage

This book would not have been possible without the help of the British Speedway Promoters
Association – particularly the Chairman Peter Toogood – as well as many promoters, fans, officials
and volunteers throughout the country too numerous to mention individually

For information on your local track and fixtures, please visit
www.british-speedway.co.uk

For some wonderful speedway action photographs, please visit
www.juliemartinphotography.co.uk
www.stevedixonphotography.co.uk

Design: Rachael Adams
www.scrutineer.co.uk
Photographs Edited by: Rachael Adams & Jeff Scott
Cover Design: Rachael Adams

UK Distributor: Central Books, 99 Wallis Road London E9 5LN 020 8986 485
www.centralbooks.com

The machinery of grace is always simple
Michael Donaghy

To
Michael Payne

Picture Editor: Rachael Adams

In its heyday, most British families would have known someone who'd visit the local Speedway track, to inhale the dust and fumes and be thrilled as they watched the boys on bikes without brakes. I visited a handful of times, trailing behind brothers to watch the Milton Keynes Knights in Bletchley. We would also watch motocross scrambling at a local farm near the Brickhill Woods. We'd come home starving, with our nostrils full of black stuff. We went banger racing too... taking for granted our exciting rural entertainment, advertised by hand-made signs strung to sign-posts, a pastime apparently free of commercialisation. Sports and events were for local communities, supported passionately without the apparent need for endorsement from television or the outside world.

Time affects even Speedway and Jeff Scott's photographs preserve its contemporary people and places. They are a vivid historical documentary archive. His photographs produce truthful, objective, and candid images from a journey taken round the United Kingdom, as he attended Speedway meetings throughout 2005 and 2006. Unguarded moments are extracted from the swirl of the event.

Hundreds and hundreds of pictures were taken with his Canon automatic digital camera – it was months into the project before Jeff discovered the flash, hence so few images taken at night! Sifting through these pictures turned out to be a joy. It's a nostalgic trip that filled me with sadness, yet also created a tremor of excitement since, once submerged in the drizzle or sunshine of these pictures, they brought back the smell, the noise, the Britishness of the sport. I combed through them: editing, juxtaposing, contrasting, scaling, cropping. And so the narrative emerged.

It's a pictorial record of us.

Photographer: Jeff Scott

You hold a book about community and tradition that masquerades as a book about Speedway. It has been spun to the periphery of Britain – geographically, culturally, historically – and no longer is the mass appeal and mainstream sport it once was. But as a consequence of this isolation, I believe Speedway has retained many of its traditional values and its charms intact. This book documents my attempt to capture the spirit of this sport through pictures of its stadiums, terraces, and people. It's a story of any Speedway meeting anywhere at any time, that moves from preparation to anticipation and beyond to a race's invariably exciting finale (albeit without the traditional action photos that other photographers do so well).

On another level, I also try to document our contemporary search for meaning and authenticity in our everyday lives. I believe that Speedway is the antithesis to most of the contemporary public spaces – places like modern shopping malls, cinemas, airports or football grounds – that dominate so many of our daily experiences and that frustrate our connection to our personal world and the people and the objects within it. We have grown more anonymous and solitary. Concepts of duty, obligation, and honour have now metamorphosed into jokes for the cynical or are seen as only instruments to coerce the gullible. But I find that I don't feel quite so miserable at the Speedway. And after I take in the atmosphere and ethos for a bit, either at my local track or round the various tracks in Britain, I notice how everyone else apparently feels as comfortable there as I do and that they believe that Speedway is worthy of their passion and commitment. Sure they still grumble and moan, but when you boil it all down, they choose to be there and take true pride in a sport with which they so closely identify.

The slightly shabby stadiums in their well-worn neighbourhoods or on industrial estates aren't as plushy plastic as most of our present, sleekly designed social spaces, which too often have a whiff of the abattoir about them. Speedway tracks always welcome you; a poster or a hand-written notice signals this far better than a business friendly mission statement or self-righteous outline of core values. As I look at these photos I notice that the people look happy, that they enjoy Speedway and embrace it for what is: a broad church where the people of its community don't pretend to be anyone that they're not. For them Speedway is a place where you can come as you are and be accepted on your own terms. Often this weekly trip to the stadium seems the most exciting event of their week and also provides a routine they can cherish for its continuity with the past.

There's something to be said for any activity that lets people delight in life any where, any time, any place; some purpose to which they can dedicate their time and effort wholeheartedly without the need for financial reward. Speedway, like many other voluntary community or cultural activities, still provides that opportunity for fulfilment, and like many other social institutions, still resists the relentless drive to consumerism, aspiration, and ambition in a world where we're continually sold comfortable, convenient, and deliberate lies. Corporations and their messages are everywhere and they have now arrived at Speedway. TV with its radioactive aura of money and power always attracts chancers, as flash as rats with gold teeth – but even with its arrival, somehow the culture of Speedway has remained immune. In fact, Speedway continues to live in a retro, more rough-hewn era of hand-written letters and genuine community rather than the more contrived world rushed by email, presented on CCTV, refined by mass marketing, ambition, or controlled by ASBOs.

You can experience so much at Speedway. You can go with your mum, your granddad, your children, your neighbours or your friends. You have an honest chance to achieve some real glamour in your life as a start-line girl, a mechanic, a helper, a rider, or as a fan. You can participate in something where the performers and all the other various people involved still recognize you or know your name. You're not as much of a statistic as you often are elsewhere. At Speedway everybody is somebody, not because they consume something because it will supposedly make them someone, but because they're part of something that resists the modern regression towards the broadest and most shallow appeal and experience possible. Upon reflection, and as I believe these photographs illustrate, Speedway simultaneously represents and fulfils our basic human need to be a member of a socially authentic community.

If you like what you see here, why not come along and share in the experience? On every night of the summer – provided it's not lashing down rain – you can watch Speedway somewhere in Britain. There must be a stadium under your nose if you will only look for it. Discover Speedway for yourself and assume your own place in this quirky but welcoming tribe that obdurately follow this most archetypically British of sports.

Contents

Shale Britannia: A Sideways Glance at Speedway

Shale Britannia: A Sideways Glance at Speedway

Shale Britannia: A Sideways Glance at Speedway

Shale Britannia: A Sideways Glance at Speedway

Shale Britannia: A Sideways Glance at Speedway

VANDALS WILL BE PROSECUTED TO THE FULL EXTENT OF THE LAW

UNDER AGE VANDALS WILL BE BANNED FROM THE STADIUM FOR 5 YEARS.

PLEASE HELP TO KEEP THESE TOILETS CLEAN

Shale Britannia: A Sideways Glance at Speedway

Shale Britannia: A Sideways Glance at Speedway

Shale Britannia: A Sideways Glance at Speedway

Shale Britannia: A Sideways Glance at Speedway

Shale Britannia: A Sideways Glance at Speedway

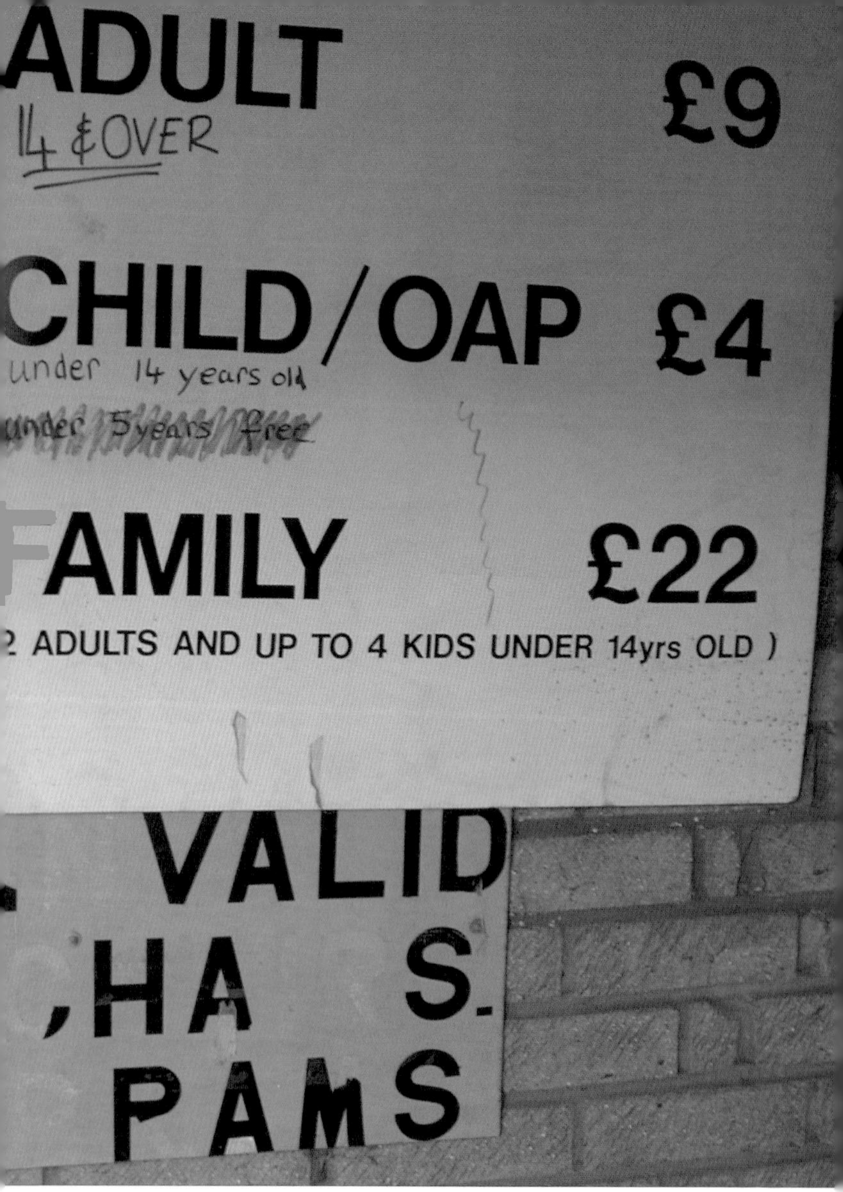

ADULT
14 & OVER

£9

CHILD/OAP
under 14 years old
under 5 years free

£4

FAMILY
(2 ADULTS AND UP TO 4 KIDS UNDER 14yrs OLD)

£22

VALID
, HA   S.
PAMS

Shale Britannia: A Sideways Glance at Speedway

Shale Britannia: A Sideways Glance at Speedway

Shale Britannia: A Sideways Glance at Speedway

Shale Britannia: A Sideways Glance at Speedway

Shale Britannia: A Sideways Glance at Speedway

Shale Britannia: A Sideways Glance at Speedway

Shale Britannia: A Sideways Glance at Speedway

Shale Britannia: A Sideways Glance at Speedway

Shale Britannia: A Sideways Glance at Speedway

Shale Britannia: A Sideways Glance at Speedway

Shale Britannia: A Sideways Glance at Speedway

Shale Britannia: A Sideways Glance at Speedway

Shale Britannia: A Sideways Glance at Speedway

Shale Britannia: A Sideways Glance at Speedway

Shale Britannia: A Sideways Glance at Speedway

THIS WAY
TO THE
BACKSTRAIGHT
ENCLOSURE
"Mick The Miler" Stand

ANDREW SAM

DANGER
THIS IS A RISK AREA
AUTHORISED PERSONS
ENTER AT THEIR OWN RISK
NO ENTRY.
PERMITTED TO.
UNAUTHORISED PERSONS

www.idealvideo.co

CO₂

Shale Britannia: A Sideways Glance at Speedway

Shale Britannia: A Sideways Glance at Speedway

Shale Britannia: A Sideways Glance at Speedway

Shale Britannia: A Sideways Glance at Speedway

Shale Britannia: A Sideways Glance at Speedway

Shale Britannia: A Sideways Glance at Speedway

Shale Britannia: A Sideways Glance at Speedway

Shale Britannia: A Sideways Glance at Speedway

Shale Britannia: A Sideways Glance at Speedway

Shale Britannia: A Sideways Glance at Speedway

| **Shale Britannia: A Sideways Glance at Speedway**

Shale Britannia: A Sideways Glance at Speedway

Shale Britannia: A Sideways Glance at Speedway

Shale Britannia: A Sideways Glance at Speedway

Shale Britannia: A Sideways Glance at Speedway

Shale Britannia: A Sideways Glance at Speedway

Shale Britannia: A Sideways Glance at Speedway

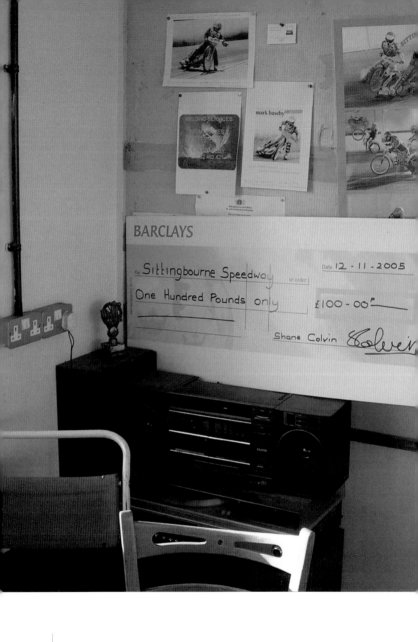

Shale Britannia: A Sideways Glance at Speedway

Shale Britannia: A Sideways Glance at Speedway

Team	No.	Team	No.	Team	No.
Swindon	9	Hull	50	Eastbourne	91
Eastbourne	10	Poole	51	Arena Essex	92
Eastbourne	11	Poole	52	Arena Essex	93
Arena Essex	12	Sittingbourne	53	Eastbourne	94
Sittingbourne	13	Poole	54	Eastbourne	95
Newcastle	14	Wimbledon	55	Arena Essex	96
Arena Essex	15	Wimbledon	56	Eastbourne	97
Poole	16	Glasgow	57	Eastbourne	98
Redcar	17	Arena Essex	58	Eastbourne	99
Arena Essex	18	Redcar	59	Arena Essex	100
Coventry	19	Isle of Wight	60	Reading	101
Eastbourne	20	Swindon	61	Wimbledon	102
Arena Essex	21	Exeter	62	Weymouth	103
Poole	22	Glasgow	63	Coventry	104
Eastbourne	23	Scunthorpe	64	Eastbourne	105
Wolverhampton	24	Belle Vue	65	Mildenhall	106
Arena Essex	25	Workington	66	Weymouth	107
Arena Essex	26	Poole	67	Eastbourne	108
Sheffield	27	Oxford	68	Arena Essex	109
Mildenhall	28	Belle Vue	69	Arena Essex	110
Sittingbourne	29	Wimbledon	70	Wimbledon	111
Mildenhall	30	Workington	71	Sittingbourne	112
Newport	31	Poole	72	Coventry	113
Sittingbourne	32	Arena Essex	73	Rye House	114
Reading	33	Isle of Wight	74	Buxton	115
Poole	34	Arena Essex	75	Workington	116
Reading	35	Coventry	76	Eastbourne	117
Redcar	36	Mildenhall	77	Reading	118
Stoke	37	Reading	78	Reading	119
Isle of Wight	38	Arena Essex	79	Stoke	120
Glasgow	39	Sheffield	80	Arena Essex	121
Mildenhall	40	Newcastle	81	Arena Essex	122
Kings Lynn	41	Belle Vue	82	Mildenhall	123
Mildenhall	42	Rye House	83	Kings Lynn	124
Coventry	43	Glasgow	84	Poole	125
Isle of Wight	44	Sittingbourne	85	Isle of Wight	126
Isle of Wight	45	Sheffield	86	Mildenhall	127
Weymouth	46	Edinburgh	87	Scunthorpe	128
Sheffield	47	Brighton	88	Isle of Wight	129
Newport	48	Swindon	89	Mildenhall	130
Plymouth	49	Eastbourne	90	Coventry	131